# What the Grimm Girl Looks Forward To

*poems by*

# Hayley Mitchell Haugen

*Finishing Line Press*
Georgetown, Kentucky

# What the Grimm Girl Looks Forward To

Copyright © 2016 by Hayley Mitchell Haugen
ISBN 978-1-63534-037-2 First Edition
All rights reserved under International and Pan-American Copyright Conventions.
No part of this book may be reproduced in any manner whatsoever without written permission from the publisher, except in the case of brief quotations embodied in critical articles and reviews.

## ACKNOWLEDGMENTS

Poems in this collection have appeared previously as follows:

After two weeks in this new bed ~ *The Southern Poetry Review*
Broken ~ *Chiron Review*
By Numbers ~ *Pearl Magazine*
Comfort ~ *Slipstream*
Fierce Calm, Flipping Mrs. Kirby ~ *Nerve Cowboy*
First Girl ~ *Ardentia Review*
Haywire ~ *One Hundred Suns* and *Wordwrights*
Inheritance ~ *Breath & Shadow*
La Loba ~ *Kaleidoscope*
mad   like dogs ~ *New Delta Review*
Mother's Milk ~ *RIPRAP* and *bite to eat place*
On Contemplating Motherhood at Dawn ~ *Inky Blue* and *Peaky Hide*
Public Appearances ~ *City Works*
Rain ~ *Poetry Northwest*
Safety ~ *Cimarron Review*
Spaces ~ *The Mid-America Poetry Review*
Summer ~ *1st & Hope*
The Girl Who Cried Lupus ~ *Wordwrights*
Trajectory ~ *Mamma Yamma*
The Wedding Photo Is Staged ~ *Beyond the Valley of the Contemporary Poets*
When we were ten ~ *Cider Press Review*
The Woman under the Bed  ~ *The Charlotte Poetry Review*
What the Grimm Girl Looks Forward To ~ *Columbia Magazine* and *Pearl*
Woman to Woman ~ *Orgasmic Grapes*


Publisher: Leah Maines
Editor: Christen Kincaid
Cover Art: David Hernandez
Author Photo: Jeffrey McClelland
Cover Design: Elizabeth Maines

Printed in the USA on acid-free paper.
Order online: www.finishinglinepress.com
also available on amazon.com

Author inquiries and mail orders:
Finishing Line Press
P. O. Box 1626
Georgetown, Kentucky 40324
U. S. A.

# Table of Contents

Introduction .................................................................. 1
Glass .......................................................................... 2
Summer ....................................................................... 3
When we were ten ...................................................... 4
Spaces ......................................................................... 6
Mother's Milk ............................................................. 7
First Girl ..................................................................... 9
On Contemplating Motherhood at Dawn ............... 10
By Numbers .............................................................. 11
Comfort .................................................................... 13
The Girl Who Cried Lupus ...................................... 14
Janine Blake where are you now ............................. 15
Haywire .................................................................... 17
Flipping Mrs. Kirby ................................................. 18
Inheritance ............................................................... 19
La Loba ..................................................................... 20
Trajectory ................................................................. 22
Safety ........................................................................ 23
Rain .......................................................................... 24
mad   like dogs ........................................................ 25
Fierce Calm ............................................................. 27
What the Grimm Girl Looks Forward To .............. 28
Woman to Woman .................................................. 29
Broken ..................................................................... 30
The wedding photo is staged .................................. 31
The Blue Wife .......................................................... 32
Public Appearances ................................................. 33
After two weeks in this new bed ............................. 34
The Woman Under the Bed .................................... 35

*For Delia,
my mother, my first reader*

# Introduction

Years ago I directed Hayley (Mitchell) Haugen's M.A. thesis. No thanks to me, it won the Best Thesis Award from the College of Liberal Arts in one of the fiercest competitions I can remember among these top scholarly and creative students from our varying disciplines, at the first great pinnacle in their lives.

Yes, she had achieved an extraordinary degree of verbal aptitude, but the true power was in her incorporation of a young lifetime of pain through the embodiment of her "Wolf" into that of the Brothers Grimm. Hers, however, she might sometimes tame to a standstill, but other times would come perilously close to being torn asunder by. She had learned, though, that her greatest weapons were her words, her intelligence, her indomitable courage, her stalwart heart, her simple refusal to succumb. Who was her enemy? Turn to poems such as "La Loba," "The Girl Who Cried Lupus," "What the Grimm Girl Looks Forward To," and "After Two Weeks in the New Bed."

After years of advanced study, university teaching, marriage, motherhood, and, always, writing—all against a background of pain—Hayley has become not just "a poet of pain." No, in my estimation she is the greatest living poet of pain with whose works I am familiar. She is, in fact, as far as I can tell, the premiere poet of her generation.

Our greatest living poet, the nonagenarian Edward Field, has said, "Only a suffering people has any virtue." Something similar may be true of individual poets. This is a woman who has brought her enemy to its knees with uncommonly brilliant artistry. I am proud beyond words of my former student, a beautiful person in all respects, Hayley (nee Mitchell) Haugen.

Gerald Locklin
Author: *The Life Force Poems*, and other works

# Glass

In fourth grade Donnia B. ran through the plate-glass
window at the New Girl's birthday party, too young
to know that doors would not always be open.
She wouldn't be back at school for months,
so we spent a week in class making bright cards
that her bandaged hands could not hold on to.

Some kids prayed for her after the pledge of allegiance.
All I knew was that she wouldn't be at recess
to *tap-tap-tap* the high bar, to beat us at nation ball,
or to eat her sack lunch with the popular kids
(one of which I was not). I could not comprehend

the thousand tiny shards of white glass needing to be plucked
out, or the stitches, like a hundred zippers holding her
together. I did not understand that she'd learned the lie early.
It was then my mother should have sat me down, told me
to pay attention to all that pain, soak it up

like the Birthday Mother's dishtowels gorged with blood,
and store it away. Maybe I would have listened,
but it was easier to let me grow up smiling
when I was told to, and not struggling,
while I went on believing life wasn't going to hurt a bit.

# Summer

Lara taught me to wear big jeans to the liquor mart
on Wednesdays, when the grandma worked the counter,
too half-blind to see the Abbazabba, Now-n-Later,

bubblegum bulge of cotton underpants.
And in our street's oak-lined cul-de-sac,
Lara showed us how to sharpen the acorns up

with that gleaming pocket knife, before twilight wars
with the Kerk brothers. And even when I was ten,
I knew what she was doing in Kobie Myer's

camper; "Go away," she said, "later, I don't
have any panties on." I knew she was bad, can
still remember Grandma Liquor chasing us

from the candy counter, both hands clutched
to her thumping heart; Bobby Kerk's right eye
squirting bright streams of blood like water

from one of those super-power pistols,
and the splintering hole Lara's stepdad kicked
smack in the middle of her bedroom door

when Kobie's mother called. But once, one summer
slumber party night, Lara taught me how to kiss
as our bodies slid and slipped in a tub of fruity

bubbles. I found parts I wasn't sure I had.
Giggles brought Mom running, and she sent Lara home,
slapped my hands until my cheeks ached, and said,

"It's wrong, it's wrong." I tried to believe,
but that night I found those parts again
and lay there, burning.

**When we were ten**

       I.

we were bold on our skinny legs, boxing with the boys,
spit dodging with the best of them, kicking up handstands
on vibrating rail-lines, our arms tense with summer muscles.

Our loose tongues were articulate, could ring out dares
no one could refuse, "chicken, chicken," hanging there,
under the slippery surface. We knew insults

and where to sling them—knew whose mother smiled
when pinched behind the grocery watermelons,
whose bottom drawers hid bags of yellow Valiums.

We knew which older sisters had clung tight
to Lawrence Russell in the high school parking lot,
half-lit by the lights of the weedy baseball diamond,

and which had made the trip to Dr. Riche's—we knew
who'd come home crying, who'd wished for scars to show
the disbelievers—and we had names for all of them.

All energy, all rolling motion, traveling beyond the reach
of our mothers' eyes, we owned our small towns, our cities.
There were no great divides, no lines of separation.

      II.

When we were twelve, we found Red-cherry Lipgloss
in our Christmas stockings and nylon stockings
in our Christmas boxes. When we ran at recess,

our little knob-breasts ached against us, our foreheads
shined, streaking our first attempts at beige foundation.
We powdered our noses with our new Avon compacts.

We packed away our Hardy Boys and Nancy Drew and turned
to Judy Blume, waiting, restless, for all she promised us.
We floated in that space between becoming young women

and remaining one of the boys. And somehow, somewhere,
we lost our language. Our tongues tied themselves up
in thick knots, so that suddenly, we needed each other.

We gaggled like geese, we blushed and giggled, we grew angry
now at the muddied centerfolds down at the creekbed.
We didn't have words for our fear, our shame,

didn't have the nerve to speak against our sisters,
couldn't remember that we ever had, or that it had always
been about power, and that somehow, we had lost it.

**Spaces**

She leaves, not pushed or overeager,
but, yes, quite casually, no room for her best shoes,
stuffed bears, or family snapshots. Outside,
there are *trees* beyond those gray freeway blocks,
lakes big enough for fish the size of T.V.s.
When she drops things now, jingling, into tight crevices,
she's surprised there is ample light to find them by the moon.
Meanwhile, her parents knock down walls to spread the silence
out between them. Mother says, come home, baby, come home;
there's so much room.

**Mother's Milk**

My sister's breasts
swell and ache
under the heavy gaze
of hungry in-laws
while her unborn child
sleeps unaware
of their expectations
their need
for that white
milky passing
of nutrients
from red, full nipples
to infant lips

Never mind
that she is scared
uninterested
or like our mother
repulsed
by thoughts of her child
sucking
like an animal
a pink piglet
in a public restroom
She is pressured to pump
lectured
as though her flow
will create the stars
fill the life giving waters
nourish all dry-mouthed babes

Deliver, sister
then take your secret pills
to dry and harden
the breasts that swing
as a burden now
Your child will never know
the difference
and your in-laws that hope
to grow fat from your milk
can afford to go
hungry awhile

## First Girl

I.

The fence is always greener on the other side
she says, so sister clambers up the cliff

where we were told not to pick raspberries high
above the blur of trains a hundred feet beneath.

Mother cautions, but just too late as Tracey slips
below low clouds, clings to vines and mudclots

rises, skinned-kneed, teary-eyed, licking berry juice
off fingers. I am the young one, no hero here,

bawling from the car door, thinking, there are times
I'd gladly knock her senseless, but not now.

II.

Let's not count our babies before they're hatched
she says, and goes to the hospital in advance.

There is so much still I don't understand, but relief
has got to drop here. Tracey sucks ice chips, twists

up bedsheets in sweaty fists, waits for the needle's
cool spinal kiss, hopes the baby will turn.

I am pillow fluffer, hand holder, peak monitor,
watching two heartbeats, counting contractions

before they hit, scared of tumbling down that edge,
and crying more when sister says, *don't watch this.*

## On Contemplating Motherhood at Dawn

At fifteen months she is good
for playing with pug-nosed dolls,
dancing to commercials,
waddling after roly-poly
blue, stuffed penguins bowled
down the hall, cute as a chick
in her yellow-fuzz Carter's
sleepwear. But Courtney screams
at 4 a.m., fills the house
with her wail, a siren,
a blue-black crow screeching,
bringing on the dawn.
I know only that she is up
and I am not, that mine
is the role of Aunt, the wand-
wielding fairy God-Mother,
who at midnight claims her right
to disappear. I ignore baby fingers
pecking at my locked door,
my name clucked out through tears.
It is easier to sink back
into feather pillows, crush
away this morning call. I can,
after all, give her nothing
of the mother, while my own
eggs I push from the nest,
let fall and break between my legs,
as warm as Saturday morning covers,
and silent.

**By Numbers**

       1

The 1s are white, you consider them first:

    your mother's fresh laundered curtains

the spatula
she's using to flip sausage squares
she'll freeze for Christmas

    the telephone
    jingling in the corner

the doctor's coat

    his chart
    with your mother's name on it

the little lab box
with a "one" in the middle

    the second hand on the kitchen clock
    making its way half-way around

       2

The 2s are orange, and of course, more difficult:

    your mother's apron
    tied gently around her waist

the coiled burners

    the skin bubble raising on your mother's wrist
    where the grease spat out and scorched her

the phone
ringing, ringing in the corner

    the glow off the doctor's scope

the "two" on the chart

    the minute hand
    jumping forward like it does
    for the fifth time

    3

The 3s are red, they bleed into everything:

    the damn phone
    screaming in the corner

the doctor's scalpel handle

    your mother, flushed
    as she pulls the chair around

the scuff it makes on the kitchen floor

    the "three,"
    circled and threatening
    on the OR schedule

the sausage
sizzling on the stove, burning itself rancid
bursting open at the seams

# Comfort

Walking home, my path is the flight of the starlings;
five hundred, five thousand, they alight, murmuring,
in each tall tree, each telephone wire to my left, to my right.
I think of what they gain in their periodic lifting,
their gathering of flocks from outlying marshes,
those leaving the protection of bridge-ledge and grove,
of what they know en route to the night spot,
where they will dive as one slick, black power
into that space of their own.

And I think of my mother, sallow with the pains
of this year, phantom ailments and the weight
of family secrets. I want to give her over to them,
raise her up to the starlings, so that she, too, can circle
above the comfort of the roost, dive headlong—
all bright beak and iridescence—into decision,
where she will sing noisily long into the night
and know what the starlings know.

# The Girl Who Cried Lupus

The town had its Alzheimer's, Parkinson's, and S.I.D.S.;
its folks had their cancers—tumors blossoming like weeds
in the best-kept flowerbeds—they had their scleroses, cirrhoses
and Psoriasis, so that when the girl grew tired on the playfields,
when she struggled up the steep hills on her rollerskates
and came home aching, they had no room
between their leukemias, their lymphomas;
they didn't want to have to name it: *Growing Pains*, they told her,
*we all went through it*. And when she was in high school
and her hair fell out—bit by thinning bit, slowly clogging up
her father's stainless steel plumbing fixtures—they worried more
about common things, the things they knew about: their ingrown toenails
and ear infections, the wart epidemic at the local spa.
Some even pointed and snickered; *Look*, they said, *she's sloughing off
like the summer dog*s. And some years later, when the mottled rash
unfurled, staining her cheeks like an unchecked leaking shoe polish,
making her look raccoon-like, wolfish, a few thought it was cute;
besides, gum disease was big then, and Down Syndrome.
They said, *Take vitamins maybe, get some sun*. Time passed
and they had their anomalies, their webbed feet and speech impediments.
They didn't seem to notice her front paws clicking down the sidewalk,
didn't look into her yellow eyes or see her tongue rolling forth
like a big pink adhesive bandage, as she sat panting
outside the local pharmaceuticals; and at night she knew,
was almost certain, that they couldn't hear her howl.

## Janine Blake, where are you now

that I can embrace you and accept your pain? Now that I awake tired and white and doped to see your face in my mirror. In sixth grade we were so afraid of your frailty: your arms bruised yellow-blue, your purple veins raised and dotted with those little round hospital Band-Aids, like key points plotted on a map. For you there was no recess or P.E. and so many excused absences the teacher stopped calling your name at roll as if you had already left us. But I could always feel you there. We made fun of you in the locker bay, locked you in like a caged animal no one wanted to touch. Laughing and jeering, the boys tried to lift your stiff brown wig with long and splintered broomsticks to see what you looked like underneath. What did you feel underneath? The class pledged allegiance to the flag, while I pledged never to end up like you. I prayed that you would quit haunting my dreams, your gray eyes staring wide and frightened out of hollow sockets like a hunted wolf. I'd wake up with headaches, convinced that I was dying, that you had looked at me the wrong way. How I wished you would die! But you followed us to High School, a living ghost in our halls. I watched as new faces taunted you, but it was getting harder to make you cry. You walked unflinching, immersed in a new world of Walkmans and books. You tuned us out, but still mourned when we lost one of our own. Was it because you would not die? Unlike Dora our freshman year, thrown from a blue moped on PCH and buried in her black Doors jacket. Did you feel the injustice like I did? I could run the track so fast with that dead girl. I had felt her power, her life, her strength as she passed off the baton. I could not accept it when you, who for years had been barely hanging on, would never know the feeling of crossing a finish line. Did you miss sports and boys? I wondered if you noticed that even Beezer would not drop pencils in geography to look up your skirt. Did you resent your mother for not letting you learn how to drive? As a senior, you showed how little these things mattered. You traded your wig for bright silk scarves and new clothes and never once looked back. I knew you had learned something we never would, and I wanted to confide in you about the aches, even then, in my bones; how I would pass out for no reason; how I was allergic to the pill. But already, you were beyond me, had learned much more about pain, had grown so quickly into a woman. Janine, did you finally die? Did you move on to college, a husband? Did you ever work or have a family of your own? Did you heal? If I should find you, I will ask; *Did you ever forgive us?* Could you ever forgive us?

## Haywire

In Vegas, my friends nickname me Haywire
and take pictures of me at that crazy slot-machine
of the same name, the white flash bouncing off
so many other swirling, noisy lights.
I am winning here, matching up fruit and brass
and dynamite on five crisscrossing lines,
so that ten, twenty, sixty silver dollars spit
jingling into my lap, and my screen rolls off
into free, unexpected spins that earn me more
and more. Like a true gambler, I exclaim
that I am reigning queen of this machine,
that I am in complete control.
Later, when I return home,
I find that my body has turned against me;
the excitement and alcohol,
the unforgiving Vegas sun was too much.
For weeks I stumble through this house
with aching joints, a circus ringing in my ears,
my periods too frequent, marking up my calendar
like a Keno board. Everything is out of order, haywire;
I can't make any of the right connections.
I awake delirious with bells and cherries in my eyes
but can't seem to get anything easy or free.
Had I known this would happen,
I would have kept one of those silver dollars
with Aladdin's curving lamp embossed on the back,
one that had come spitting out, all cockeyed and haywire.
I'd rub the lamp, get back on track, conjure up
that spinning, winning feeling of complete control.
But of course I cashed all those coins in,
traded my charms and tokens for the real thing,
forgot that there is no control, that life is in that lamp,
so much wishful thinking.

**Flipping Mrs. Kirby**

Nana took three weeks to die while we sat silent
in bright terminal ward corners, waiting,
cringing as needles slipped in to the tops
of wrinkled sunspots, her hands so thin and dry
we thought they'd snap like Mom's burnt Sunday bacon.
Her hair falling out in straight silver threads
on her pillowcase, Nana lay still, a single
perfect jaundiced line, fading each day
like a Highlighting marker on a too white page.
Quiet. Her death so light, so easy.

Not like Mrs. Kirby, who lay rotund in the next
bed, moaning deep from her thick throat
when male nurses came to flip her each morning.
Neck folds wet with sweat, a walrus in the heat,
when they pushed from her legs, her top took moments
more to catch the motion. Then, her gigantic buttocks
jiggling, displaying the horrors of bed sores,
raised red and bursting from all that weight,
that noisy pain.

Years later now, I sometimes wake with fists clenched
tight as knotted rope. Fingers needing stretching,
a straightening out, legs bent up like boxed calves,
I am pulled and prodded into each damp day. Head weak,
seeming like I'll float away, I think of Mrs. Kirby,
heavy with knowing what was killing her, and I realize
no one simply fades. Even Nana, disappearing into bedsheets,
must have felt it, death sitting dense on brittle ribs,
waiting to strangle the last breath from her day.

## Inheritance

      I.

Great Aunty Sissy's amber beads are packed
haphazardly in Mother's jewelry box—
a cardboard affair, gray tape curling up
on two squashed sides—the gold chain tangling
itself amongst tarnished Disney charms; the yellow
curative glass scratching up against vending machine
mood rings as if it didn't know any better.

      II.

My mother has been ill for weeks, the dark cloud
of diagnosis hanging over all of us as we wait
for test results. When they tell her it's Lupus,
I am relieved, it seems, more so than the others.
I say, *Welcome to the wolf pack;* this is something
we've dealt with. She thinks though, that I will use this
against her, blame, a new theme in my poems.

      III.

The beads, we've figured, are antique now,
from the 1890's when Sissy was in her teens.
I suggest an appraisal, but my mother hesitates,
asks, *You wouldn't ever sell them would you?*
as though I can't picture fat Aunty Sissy dancing
at age eighteen; as though I don't feel the same dull ache
that burrows in my mother's bones; as though I don't know
what I, too, may pass along, to my own unborn daughters,
and they to theirs, forever.

**La Loba**
> *(after Clarissa Pinkola Estes)*

Search deep in the mountains,
the arid arroyos, the parched
river beds of the flat plains,
and you will find her, the Wild
Woman, wolf woman, *La Loba*.

She walks the wilds, collects
bones, bit by bit, in a woven
basket strapped to her hunching back.
She preserves that which
is in danger of being lost.

Her cave, a museum, a gallery
of bones, smooth white sculptures,
is full of desert creatures: rattlesnakes,
crows, and wolves, her specialty. Once
assembled, full skeletons laid out

before her, she stands and sings.
Her voice carried by the wind, rustles
the mountain pines, stirs up the dunes
into flurries of dust. Her beasts awaken.
Wolf bones regain flesh and fur,

become strong, and suddenly breathe
life. Howling, the canine's song is
Wild Woman's, and the dog, delivered
into the night, leaps up, and escapes
its mother's den. Something, the speed

of its race, its breath smoking out
into the chilled night air, a drop
of rain, or a beam of moon, hitting
it just right, transforms the wolf
into a woman, laughing, a wolf-woman,
who runs free into the glowing horizon.

*La Loba* is the keeper of my soul,
the guardian of the illness that
threatens my strength and sanity.
For a year she's been inside me,
collecting bones, so that I won't

lose my shape. At first I didn't
understand, I feared the wolf that
she was building. I feel its toenails
digging in my brain, and I awake to
clumps of hair, lost to my pink pillow.

Its wolf ribs tangle with my own, weigh
heavy in my chest, steal my breath, condemn
me to a week of pleurisy. As the beast matures,
I am plunged into new stages, the bridge
of its nose nudging my kneecaps, leaving

me weak and arthritic, so that I curse
*La Loba*. But now, her puzzle of bones
is complete, and I have seen the worst
of everything. The wolf has become a part
of me, and I've gained its instinct.

I have seen my weaknesses, have learned
when not to venture out. Soon I will hear
La Loba singing, my wolf howling. I will
know all, and I will run free, and laughing
into the horizon, a wolf-woman, *La Loba*.

## Trajectory

On the wide streets of Anchorage, no fences
between houses, our small worlds tumbled together.
When Bernadette streaked through the neighborhood
each snowy December, we wiped the condensation
from our living-room windows and watched
as one face watching.

For the game home from the bus-stop, we molested
the curbside mailboxes, raised red metal flags
in a show of patriotism, and mixed up the bills
amongst the neighbors. When we were cruel,
we'd leave hand-scrawled messages from forgotten
relatives: mothers who'd run off with office clerks,
husbands who'd smashed themselves up in weekend binges.

In the spring we skipped the school bus altogether, cut
through the Baptist churchyard in our galoshes
and crinkling rain-suits, barely breathing, gesturing quietly
with airport hand signals. Inside we had spied the minister
in his knee-high fishing boots, drowning the sinners
in a tank as wide as the downtown movie screen.

One full summer, someone shot the dogs at night.
We'd wake in the middle of dreams to that familiar echo,
calculate distance, trajectory, like men on the Bowling league
figuring if the ball would strike. In the mornings we'd find dogs
bleeding, or others that had jumped, scared from the balconies,
and hanged themselves.

When the next first snow fell, Bernadette made
an early statement; she came out jogging in a red leather collar,
the Peterson's Chihuahua yapping circles around her bare ankles.
We wiped the condensation from our living-room windows,
and we watched, with something like terror and amusement.

# Safety

Driving in Boston, we hear again the news from California:
forest fires, earthquakes, drive-by shootings; the newsman
is incredulous. Why do we live there, just dangling,
it seems, so high on the nation's list of most dangerous places?
And David gives me the look, confirms his hatred of the place
I've displaced him to. He gestures wide to the trees surrounding us,
but I lack faith in our survival skills; we would be lost out there.
A truck idles to a stop next to us. In its bed is a mini camper shell
divided into pens. There are greyhounds inside, muzzled, their snouts
pressed to the mesh screen windows. I can hear them whining,
whimpering; I don't feel safer here.

Back home, my sister is driving to the hospital. Someone may
throw a brick through her windshield, but it is unlikely.
She is doing a psych-ward rotation, working with the violent ones
in lockdown. They are not going anywhere, but still, she has forgotten
to tape up her student badge to cover her last name—just in case
they get out and remember her, what they liked, or didn't.
She plays ping-pong with Bob, who calls her by her full name.
He's thirty, seems like a nice guy, she says. At the end of the week
she reads his files, finds he strangled his father with his bathrobe tie.

More and more, I am feeling that I would rather stay in.
It's like I know the streets will be too crowded—people in a constant
state of preparation, but I don't know what for. Everywhere,
they are taking stock, keeping an eye on things, like some big news
is about to break, something even the smallest of us feel.
On my way to the grocery store, the driver in the beat up impala behind me
is lifting weights. He gets in a quick right arm set with a good-sized
    dumbbell
before the lights change, then accelerates, continues with his left.
As he passes me, I notice his little girl in the back seat. She has propped up
a giant-sized book on her bare knees. She is working on an angel,
holding her high as she colors her black, black wings.

**Rain**
    *(for William Shadden)*

This summer I take twenty kids, young poets with pencils
as sharp as hope in their pockets, to see
an African storyteller, a musician, on campus.

He shows us instruments we've never seen,
whose vibrations shake the stiff academic halls.
He bids us push the tables aside, stand,
stomp our feet, slap hands and thighs and hips
with one, two, four partners, raise our white middle-class voices
and sing a Ugandan children's song.

There is only one girl, one long blonde braid and thick glasses,
who will not participate, who looks at me as if I, her teacher,
should know better. She does not latch on, like I do, to the lilting words
of the storyteller, this stranger who tells me that in Africa,
the dead are not dead, they just go away.

I shake the gourd rattles, and in my shaking,
she does not see I speak to you. The classroom
fills with the rhythm of rain, but she does not dance in it
as I do, does not understand my tears.
She will not let down that thick braid when her family,
all she knows, is safe at home.

She does not need this fake rain, but I use it,
open my mouth, even, to catch the drops;
use it to remember Winter Break spent under your umbrella,
your covers; I recall your car, the wipers squeaking
as you drove to school with one hand on my knee;

I use it, like the shekere in Africa, to speak with the dead,
and to awaken here, this little girl amongst the living.

**mad   like dogs**


it is august in big bear and your friend is still dead
three months gone     down the mountain in a city
without wildflowers

so you hike with two others youre not sure
you know now and maybe never did     you hike without water
or the widebrimmed hat the doctor ordered

you hope youll get sunstroke              you pick strange plants
bend close to obvious snakeholes       at an arid plateau
you discover a carcass    a charred and leafless tree

split like a V or a hand upstretched for water     you take off
your tshirt     your bra     you climb the stump and pose
on it with the woman    you hope lightning will strike twice

in the distance you hear lowflying helicopters
you want them to see you       you want to get arrested
the man takes pictures in black & white

back home you will not know whats become
of them       it rains at the cabin     thick cold drops
that sting your weathered arms

you jump around in them     crave sudden pneumonia
in the middle of the street     imagine no brakes     a red
diesel engine slamming into you

it feels so good   you dry off with a bottle
of bitter wine          smoke a joint with the cabin owners
you skid down the carpeted stairs on your ass

like a child            you hope to break your neck
at the bottom         the others follow your lead
you hope theyll crush you      finish you off

you join in a ruckus         a contest of sorts
on the balcony        the railing is fragile       untrustworthy
you pray the whole scene will collapse

into the coyotes below    you yelp at the cliche moon
cup your hands around your chapped lips
and howl        and you think youve done it

you think youve got them beat          you think that
all the eyes in the night cant see you are the same woman
you think the dead can hear you

## Fierce Calm

When the Chevy rounds the corner,
one wheel spinning on air,
when it skids through the stop sign
and I see the muscular man
riding the truck's back fender,
hear his drunken whooping in the pre-dawn light,
I know I am as close to danger, as near
that deep abyss of imperfect human decision
as I have ever been, when what we do
or don't, this man and I, means everything.
And I remain, a woman alone in her car
at 5am—keys in the ignition, lights off,
making all the difference—I sit in terror
and wonder. And I just *know* to not get out,
that it's not my weaker sex, that it's not paranoia,
that it has nothing to do with not being polite
or brave to fold myself into the seats,
to disappear into the floorboards, to whisper,
*I am not here, I am not here, I am not
here.*

## What the Grimm Girl Looks Forward To

My birth will kill my seven brothers,
turn them into ravens, into stones.
My parents will hate me, cut off my hands
for the devil behind the watershed.

Or the brothers will live and be valiant,
skillful, faithful, Iron men, and I,
the ugly one, sent to fetch water
in heavy, pewter buckets full of holes.

There will be frogs everywhere.

I will be orphaned in a paper frock,
left to the forest of wizards and gnomes.
My stepmother will be evil, will hammer
me into barrels, imprison me in thorns.

If I am beautiful, they'll call me idle.
If I am smart enough to see the wind come
up the street, they'll say I am proud. If I am
obstinate or inquisitive, they'll take me
for a block of wood and throw me in the fire.

I will waste my youth spinning straw to gold.

If my flax remains unknotted I will find
a husband, but I will be stupid, will fall
into wells. I will roll cheese down hills to catch
my fallen crackers. I will hang cow bells
around my neck to be sure I am heading home.

I will become greedy. Tempted to bathe
myself in milk, I will sell my sons
for silver coins. I will wake up wrinkled,
an apple, an old and lonely crone.
And still, it will not be enough.

I will open that thirteenth door.

## Woman to Woman
*(when I see trouble and you are blind)*

I want to be one of the two-inch gargoyles
suspended from your curtain rod,
want to hide amongst your black silk sheers
wide-eyed, watching for the first time
your perfect white skin and fashion sense
without jealousy, without words, lectures,
without that need to call you sister, friend.
I want to protect without your knowing,
cast spells, an evil eye on the man you can't love
without alcohol, the man who pulls your hair,
fills your ears with songs of love, then drains you
inch by inch until you crack dry and bleed.
I want to bite his ankles, his penis
with poisoned teeth, prevent him from thrusting
from driving himself into you, confusing you,
making you want, making you dream
of the babies you think you need. I want to shatter
your silence with my own piercing gargoyle cry,
populate his nightmares, force him to acknowledge
my watching, my sitting, ugly and threatening,
your guardian against evil influences.

**Broken**

If we were men,
we'd have worked
this out by now.
We'd trade power
tools, you offering
the use of your radial
arm saw for my new
*Black & Decker* drill.
We'd give up some
push for some pull,
rebuild the structure
that has started to
crumble between us,
hammer problems out,
extract the rusting
nails imbedded in
the wood. We'd mend
things with a little
sweat and exchange
of power. But instead
we pull each other tight
as guitar strings,
collect grievances,
and wind them up like
old clocks bursting
at the springs, never
allowed to relax and
uncurl. We ignore the
things about to snap,
rather than fix them
like men, with tools
we are too proud
to borrow.

## The wedding photo is staged

you have seen this before: bride facing hotelroom mirror,

focused, her white veil flowing like the long road
of the American dream beyond her chair, beyond the picture.

Her pearls hang proud as picket fences around her neck,
soften at exposed borders of talcumed breasts, the diamonds

swinging loosely from ears whisper, *Yes, you've made it.*
Though their real bodies are cropped, insubstantial

in the frame, mother and sister reflect approval in the glass.
The mood is smiles—the same three smiles—the air

all freesia, pink roses, and baby's-breath. You don't know,
that very morning, the mother arrived panicked and screeching,

quieting laughter between sisters once again, as in the days
of shared bath times and slumber parties,

that the bride's sequined gown will be spilt on, torn;
her back will ache with dancing; the groom will flirt

with her best friend; she'll get short-sheeted;
or that the sister will sleep next to a man who hasn't made love

to her in six months, and still won't, despite the free room,
the cool spring evening, the fact that she caught the bouquet.

**The Blue Wife**

read a story once about a woman
who walked into a cornfield, just left
her gaping husband at a roadside Super-quick
and strolled into the embrace of night,
the fireflies closing the gaps behind her,
briefly lighting the spaces she had been.

Blue Wife, though, is no romantic: the forest
behind her house slowly encroaches,
all coyote howl and jaw bone, deer tic
and smothering kudzu. Poison ivy strangles
her shrubbery, darkens the sun porch walls,
and the hope that is the firefly, is too fleeting
to light the way.

**Public Appearances**
    *(for Lisa Glatt)*

At the bookstore in San Pedro
he approaches us, asks,
may I take pictures
while you are reading?
We think, Press? Reviewer?
Poet stalker? Freak?
He looks harmless enough.
We ask, where will they end up?
Oh, you know, he says, nowhere,
they may sit, undeveloped.
We are dubious. We don't encourage him.
When we read, we hold our heads down
as he peers through the eyepiece;
we don't smile, don't articulate
in his direction, but wonder
if they are black and white
and if our noses are shining.
At the end of the evening,
as we try to escape,
he corners us,
asks for headshots. *Together*,
we insist, pulling close, as women do.
*Closer*, he says, and it is then
we feel it, resent being captured
in the black box he will take home with him.
*This is the one I shot Ginsberg with*,
he says, the zoomlens pulsing
towards us, heavy in his eager, guiding hand.
We stiffen against each other,
control our laughter or anger.
We think of the words of our poems
swirling through his head:
*vagina, breast, one large ball;*
we wonder what he'll do with them.

### After two weeks in this new bed
*(for Cat Spydell)*

I am tempted to let the blood run free when it comes,
a wolf lost from the pack, I need to impress
upon the space that has become mine. I think of a friend
in Mendocino, how even the thick trees closing in
around her small cabin, like a thousand different faces
in a new city, do not make her anonymous.

She climbs to the roof, she says, screams into the forest,
bare breast to naked sun; she has a voice.
With each new cycle of blood
vultures circle high above her garden, raccoons forage
deeper into the dumpster at the side gate.
The animals keep their distance though, while she bleeds
or gives birth, becomes a part of them
a world away from the city life she is used to.

Here, there is only one big tree outside my window,
and the squirrels that skitter around the grassy apartment quad
are quick to move for anyone. My flannel sheets
are comforting enough, warm as the California sun
I've left behind, but this spring mattress is hard
beneath me, does not give when my breasts swell.

Forced to sleep on my side, I awake stiff
and cranky, feeling as though I should have gained
something from the discomfort: a child, respect,
a new take on the landscape. My four morning walls
offer no room to move, no green oxygen
to breathe, when all I want to do is climb
to the top and scream, and bleed over everything.

## The Woman Under the Bed
*(after Erica Jong, an imitation)*

The woman under the bed
The woman who has been there forever recording my life
The woman who records each toss and choice of clothing
The woman who is still as floorboards settled into the darkness
The woman whose whisper is the whispering of small pale door mice
The woman whose whispering raises the hairs on my neck
The woman in the garden whose whisper wilts the wildflowers
The witchwoman in corners who spirals through spiderwebs
The woman at the bottom of the bottom of the barrel

I met her tonight     I always meet her
She stands in the evening light of the train station
When the whistles screech like circling crows
& coach doors slam open like coffin lids
When I am smothered by crowds & close to drowning
she pulls her black silk from around her features
she smiles toothless and reeking
For years she has wanted to stake a claim
& now she says
She has only wanted me to retain her image
We stroll through the tunnels like May & December
We rise through the floor of the floor of my room

If she is my destiny she will return curled into my torso
Her whisper will weave messages in the lines of my eyelids
I will bend into her contours like the warp of the floorboards
I will whisper into her ears
& conceive her whole

Hayley Mitchell Haugen holds a Ph.D. in 20th Century American Literature from Ohio University and an MFA in poetry from the University of Washington. She is currently Associate Professor of English at Ohio University Southern, where she teaches courses in composition, American literature, and creative writing. Her poetry has appeared or is forthcoming, in *Nerve Cowboy, Poetry Northwest, Rattle, Slant, Spillway,* and many other journals. Critical essays appear in *The Body in Medical Culture; On the Literary Nonfiction of Nancy Mairs;* and *Stephen King's Contemporary Classics: Reflections on the Modern Master of Horror,* and elsewhere.

www.ingramcontent.com/pod-product-compliance
Lightning Source LLC
LaVergne TN
LVHW041551070426
835507LV00011B/1037